Fall

by Tanya Thayer

first step nonfiction

It is fall.

It is getting colder.

The days are shorter.

Children go back to school.

Leaves change color.

Children play in leaves.

Squirrels **store** nuts.

People store food.

Animals eat **berries.**

People pick apples.

Pumpkins grow big.

Seeds grow big.

Flowers start to die.

Frost covers plants.

Geese fly south.

Winter is coming.

Seasons

The earth moves around the
sun. The sun shines on the
earth. When the sun shines
mostly on the middle of the
earth, it is fall in the United
States.

There is less sunlight in the fall
than there is in the summer.
The days are shorter in the fall,
too. When there is less sunlight
in a day, it is colder.

Fall Facts

Another word for fall is autumn.

Fruit becomes ripe in the fall. People and animals eat fruit and seeds. Seeds left on the ground will make new plants in the spring.

When birds fly from cold parts of the world to warmer parts of the world it is called migration. Warmer parts of the world have more food than colder parts. Birds migrate in the fall.

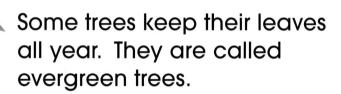

Some trees lose their leaves in the fall. They are called deciduous trees.

Some trees keep their leaves all year. They are called evergreen trees.

Animals need to eat a lot of food in the fall. Their bodies make fat from the food they eat. Their fat will keep them warm in the winter.

Glossary

 berries – the fruit of a bush

 flowers – the part of a plant that makes seeds

 frost – crystalized water

 leaves – the part of a plant that makes food

 store – to keep for later use